30 Delicious Refrigerator Cake Recipes

That Will Make You Go "Mmmmm"

By

LORI BURKE

Legal Stuff

First Printing: 2012

ISBN-13: 978-1470123680

ISBN-10: 1470123681

Printed in the United States of America

DEDICATION

For Mom:

Every time I cook I think of you.

Love,

Lori

CONTENTS

Introduction

Hi There!

Welcome to my little book of cakes. I wanted to share with you how I became interested in refrigerator cakes.

One day when I was a little girl Mom said she was going to show me how to make a special cake. I was surprised. Since Mom worked, she only baked when there was a holiday or a birthday. This was just an average Saturday morning. So I watched with curiosity as she brought out a round cake pan, two boxes of vanilla wafers and a bunch of bananas.

Mom asked me to fill the bottom of the pan with a row of vanilla wafers. While I did that she peeled and sliced a banana. Then she put a banana slice on each vanilla wafer. "This is a cake?" I asked, wondering if it was a trick to get me to eat more fruit. "Just wait and see," Mom replied.

I put another layer of vanilla wafers over the bananas in the pan. Mom followed with more bananas. We kept at it until we had five layers of cookies and bananas with a final layer of vanilla wafers on top. Then Mom wrapped the cake with plastic wrap and put it in the refrigerator. I remember thinking that this was not going to be a very good cake.

That night after dinner Mom took the cake out of the refrigerator and put it on the counter. She took a can of Reddi-Wip® and covered the top of the cake with whipped cream. Then she cut three pieces and set one plate in front of my Dad and one plate in front of me. Dad looked at me. I looked at Dad. We had never seen a dessert like this before. We picked up our forks and dug in.

I still remember the wonderful taste of soft cold vanilla cookie cake with sweet bananas and even sweeter Reddi Wip® all melting in my mouth. "This is great!" I said. All Dad said (over and over) was "Mmmmmm" as he inhaled the cake. Mom just smiled and ate her cake. That was when I was first introduced to the wonderful world of refrigerator cakes.

Refrigerator cakes were originally created with cookies, fruit and whipped cream. They were also called icebox cakes or no-bake cakes. Then bakers spread their wings and got more creative. They started incorporating cake rather than cookies as the base. Some of these later refrigerator cakes are called "Poke Cakes." Bakers would poke holes into the top of the cake and drizzle a delicious topping so that it would seep into the holes. Add whipped cream, fruit and nuts and you had a little piece of heaven.

In this cookbook I've collected refrigerator cake recipes that I have found to be the BEST. The collection includes 24 traditional refrigerator cakes and 6 Poke cakes. The refrigerator cakes are fast and easy to prepare. The Poke cakes require a little bit more baking but are so delicious!

I hope you enjoy these cakes as much as my family and I do!

Lori Burke

A Note for the Health-Conscious

Some of these recipes call for whipped cream, heavy cream, butter, eggs, sugar or cream cheese. For those of you attempting to lose weight or who are trying to live in a heart-healthy way, there are some ways to reduce the fat and calories in these cakes.

Substitutions

1. Use fat-free sweetened condensed milk instead of regular condensed milk

2. Use fat-free vanilla wafers instead of regular vanilla wafers

3. Whenever sugar is called for you can use a combination of ½ sugar and ½ SPLENDA

4. Use low-fat cream cheese instead of regular cream cheese

5. Use low-fat COOL WHIP instead of regular COOL WHIP

6. Use skim milk instead of regular milk

7. Garnish cakes with fresh fruit instead of chocolate or nuts

The above substitutions will reduce the fat content of the cakes. But they will still be delicious and wonderful desserts!

Amrita Refrigerator Cake

Ingredients

- 1 1/2 cups graham cracker crumbs
- 3 tablespoon sugar, divided
- 2 packages pineapple gelatin (3 oz. each)
- 1 cup oranges, diced
- 1 can coconut (4 oz.)
- 1 cup heavy cream
- 2 cup boiling water
- 1 can crushed pineapple, undrained (20 oz.)
- 1/4 cup butter, melted

Directions

1. Mix together graham cracker crumbs, 2 tablespoons sugar, and melted butter. Press the mixture into the bottom of a 13" x 9" pan. Set aside.
2. Mix pineapple gelatin and boiling water in a bowl. Make sure the gelatin is dissolved.
3. Add the pineapple and oranges and stir well. Chill until slightly thickened.
4. Add 1 cup coconut and mix well.
5. Whip the heavy cream with the remaining 1 tablespoon sugar. Fold into the gelatin mixture.
6. Pour the gelatin onto the prepared crust.
7. Chill until firm.
8. Toast remaining coconut to use as garnish before serving.

Banana Cream Icebox Cake

Ingredients

- 35 chocolate wafer cookies
- 3 tablespoons confectioners' sugar
- 3 tablespoons semisweet-chocolate pieces
- 1 teaspoons vanilla extract
- 2 small bananas, ripe, diced (1 ½ cups)
- 2 cups heavy or whipping cream

Directions

1. Combine the heavy cream, vanilla and sugar in a bowl and beat with a mixer until stiff peaks form. Reserve half of the whipped cream and refrigerate.
2. Slowly fold the bananas into remaining whipped cream.
3. Spread 2 teaspoons of the banana cream mixture on one side of each of 6 chocolate wafers. Create a small tower by stacking the wafers on top of each other. Put a seventh plain wafer on the top.
4. Create 5 more stacks of wafers and banana cream.
5. Turn each stack on its side; Place each stack side by side on a large platter so that the rounded edges of the wafers are next to each other. It will resemble a log.
6. Frost the log with the reserved whipped cream and sprinkle the chocolate pieces on top.
7. Cover and refrigerate at least 4 so that the wafers soften.

Banana Refrigerator Cake

Ingredients

- 1 box vanilla wafers
- 2 large boxes of cook and serve Chocolate pudding
- Coconut or chopped nuts
- 6 large bananas

Directions

1. Cook pudding according to directions and set aside to cool.
2. Place a layer of vanilla wafers in the bottom of a 13" x 9" pan.
3. Spread a layer of sliced bananas over the cookies
4. Spread 1/2 the pudding over the bananas
5. Repeat layers ending with the pudding
6. Sprinkle with coconut and / or chopped nuts
7. Keep refrigerated

Banana Split Poke Cake

Ingredients

- 1 package banana cake mix
- 1 package strawberry JELL-O gelatin dessert (3 ounce)
- water

Topping

- 1 envelope DREAM WHIP whipped topping
- 1 box chocolate instant pudding (3 1/2 ounce)
- 1 1/2 cups cold milk

Directions

1. Preheat oven to 350
2. Dissolve the JELL-O in ¾ cup boiling water and stir well. Stir in ½ cup cold water.
3. Mix and bake cake as directed on package for a 13"x 9" pan.
4. Cool cake 20-25 minutes.
5. Use a skewer or the handle of a small wooden spoon to poke deep holes into the top of the warm cake. Holes should be 1 inch apart.
6. Pour the JELL-O mixture over the cake making sure JELL-O goes into the holes. Refrigerate the cake.
7. Chill a bowl and blend the topping ingredients. Beat until stiff and fluffy.
8. Frost the cake with the DREAM WHIP topping.
9. Garnish with strawberry and banana slices.
10. Store in refrigerator and serve chilled.
11. Can be frozen for storage.

Variation

You can substitute COOL WHIP for the whipped topping

Brandy Almond Refrigerator Cake

Ingredients

Cake

- 2 cup powdered sugar
- 1 cup toasted almond slivers
- 1 large angel food cake
- 1 cup butter, softened
- 5 egg yolks
- 1/2 cup Brandy

Frosting

1. 1 pint heavy cream, whipped
2. 1/4 cup Brandy
3. 1/2 teaspoon Vanilla
4. 3 to 4 tablespoons powdered sugar

Directions

Cake

1. Butter a skillet and sauté the almond slivers until lightly browned. Set aside to cool.
2. In a bowl blend the butter with sugar. Beat until fluffy.
3. Add in egg yolks, one at a time, beating well after each yolk.
4. Add in the brandy and almonds. Mix well.
5. Line a rounded bowl with waxed paper.
6. Slice the angel food cake in layers 1/2 inch thick.
7. Place a layer of cake on the bottom of the bowl, then a layer of brandy mixture.
8. Continue in this order until all brandy mixture is used and bowl is filled.
9. Chill overnight. Transfer to a serving plate and frost.

Frosting

1. Combine the heavy whipped cream, brandy, vanilla and powdered sugar in a bowl and beat on high speed for at least 10 minutes or until fluffy. Frost the cake and chill in the refrigerator

Chocolate Banana Refrigerator Cake

Ingredients

- 1 package JELL-O Chocolate Instant Pudding (3.9 ounce)
- 1 cup cold milk
- 1 tub COOL WHIP Whipped Topping, thawed, divided (8 ounce)
- 1 banana, chopped
- 11 NABISCO Honey Maid Honey Grahams, broken in half, divided

Directions

1. Beat pudding mix and milk in a medium bowl with an electric mixer or hand whisk until well blended (1 to 2 minutes)
2. Stir 1-1/2 cups COOL WHIP and bananas into the pudding mixture.
3. Spread 1 Tablespoon pudding mixture onto each of 20 graham squares.
4. Stack graham crackers together, and then stand on edge on serving platter to make 8-1/2-inch loaf.
5. Frost with remaining COOL WHIP. Crush remaining graham squares; sprinkle over loaf.
6. Refrigerate 4 hours.

Variation

Add walnuts on top

Chocolate Vanilla Refrigerator Cake

Ingredients

- 3 boxes French vanilla instant pudding (3/4 ounce)
- 3 cups milk
- 1 container COOL WHIP (8 ounce)
- 1 box graham cracker
- 2 tablespoons butter
- 2 tablespoons corn syrup
- 1 1/2 cups confectioners' sugar
- 2 (1 ounce) unsweetened baking chocolate melted and cooled

Directions

1. Combine pudding and milk. Mix until thick.
2. Fold the COOL WHIP into the pudding.
3. Put a layer of graham crackers on the bottom of a 9" x 13" Pyrex pan. Top with a layer of pudding.
4. Continue creating layers of graham crackers and pudding until there are no more graham crackers
5. In a saucepan, heat the corn syrup and butter.
6. Sift the confectioner's sugar into the corn syrup – butter mixture
7. Mix thoroughly and add the melted chocolate.
8. Use the Chocolate-Sugar-Corn Syrup mixture to frost the last layer of Graham Crackers. Add a little milk to the frosting mixture if needed.
9. Chill in the refrigerator overnight.

Chocolate Peanut Butter Refrigerator Cake

Ingredients

- 10 ounces peanut butter chips
- 18 chocolate graham crackers
- 2 1/2 cups heavy cream

Directions

1. Use a microwave safe bowl to heat 2/3 cup cream until steaming.
2. Add the peanut butter chips to the hot milk and whisk until smooth.
3. Slowly whisk in remaining cream. Chill for 15 minutes.
4. Remove the peanut butter mixture from the refrigerator.
5. Beat the peanut butter mixture with a mixer until soft peaks form.
6. Place 3 crackers, side by side, long edges touching on the bottom of a serving plate. Spread 1/2 cup of the cream mixture on top of the crackers. Add 4 more layers of crackers and cream mixture; add 1 more layer of crackers on top of the cake.
7. Chill the cake for 1 hour.
8. Chill the remaining cream. Spread the top and sides of the cake with remaining cream.
9. Chill the cake for 4 hours.
10. Decorate the top of the cake with peanut butter chips.

Coco Lopez Refrigerator Poke Cake

Ingredients

- 1 box white cake mix (18 ounce)
- Egg whites (Use the amount specified in the cake mix directions)
- Oil   (Use the amount specified in the cake mix directions)
- Water   (Use the amount specified in the cake mix directions)
- 1 can EAGLE Brand Condensed Milk (14 ounce)
- 1 can COCO LOPEZ (cream of coconut) (8 1/2 ounce)
- coconut
- 1 carton COOL WHIP (9 ounce)

Directions

1. Bake the cake according to directions 9" x 13" pan.
2. Mix the EAGLE Brand Condensed Milk
3. Poke holes in cake while hot using a meat fork.
4. Pour the condensed milk – COCO LOPEZ mixture over the cake and let cool completely.
5. Frost with COOL WHIP and top with coconut.
6. Refrigerate.

Variations

- Use fat free sweetened condensed milk and fat free COOL WHIP.
- Sprinkle the top with shredded coconut

Coconut Refrigerator Poke Cake

Ingredients

Cake

- 1 box yellow cake mix (18 1/4 ounce)
- 1 1/4 cups water
- 1/3 cup vegetable oil
- 3 eggs

Syrup

- 1 1/2 cups sugar
- 1 cup milk (Low-fat is fine.)
- 1 teaspoon coconut flavoring

Topping

- 1 container COOL WHIP (8 ounce)
- Coconut , toasted

Directions

1. Preheat oven to 350 degrees.
2. Spray a 13" x 9" inch pan with cooking spray and flour lightly.
3. Prepare the cake mix using the water, oil and eggs as directed on package directions.
4. Bake in preheated oven as directed on package.
5. Bring the sugar and milk to a boil over medium heat; stir in coconut flavoring and remove from heat.
6. Remove the cake from the oven when it's done.
7. While the cake is hot use the handle of a wooden spoon to poke holes in the top of the cake.
8. Pour the coconut syrup over the top of the hot cake and allow to cool to room temperature.

9. Cover and refrigerate until serving time.
10. When you're ready to serve the cake frost the cake with COOL WHIP and sprinkle with lightly toasted coconut.

German Chocolate Icebox Cake

Ingredients

- 8 (1 ounce) squares German sweet chocolate, chopped
- 3 tablespoons water
- 2 egg yolks, beaten
- 2 tablespoons confectioners' sugar
- 1 cup heavy whipping cream
- 2 egg whites
- 1 package ladyfingers (12 ounce)

Directions

1. Line two 8 x 4 x 3 inch loaf pans with waxed paper.
2. Beat the whipping cream until soft peaks form.
3. Beat the egg whites until stiff.
4. Melt the chocolate in a double boiler and blend in water. Remove from heat and add the egg yolks. Beat vigorously until smooth and blended.
5. Add sugar to the chocolate mixture and mix well.
6. Fold whipped cream into the chocolate mixture.
7. Fold the stiffly beaten egg whites into the chocolate mixture.
8. Separate the ladyfingers. Line bottom of each pan with a single layer of ladyfingers.
9. Cut the remaining ladyfingers in half crosswise and use to line the sides of the pans.
10. Fill each pan with the chocolate mixture.
11. Chill 12 to 24 hours. Unmold. Serve with additional whipped cream if desired.

Variations

- Top the cake with fresh whipped cream or fruit or chocolate shavings or semi-sweet chocolate chips or walnuts.
- Use chocolate wafer cookies instead of ladyfingers
- Use an OREO crust instead

Happy Holidays Refrigerator Cake

Ingredients

- 1 cup chopped candied cherries
- 1 cup chopped candied pineapple
- 1 cup dates, pitted and chopped
- 1 cup chopped salted pecans
- 1/2 pound marshmallows, quartered
- 1 cup cream
- 1 cup graham cracker crumbs
- 2 teaspoons orange zest
- 2 teaspoons sherry
- 1 cup whipped cream

Directions

1. Combine the cream and marshmallows in a saucepan over low heat. Keep folding the cream and marshmallow mixture over and over until the marshmallows are partially melted. Remove the pan from heat and keep on folding until the mixture is smooth. Set aside to cool.
2. Add the fruit, orange zest, nuts, 3/4 cup graham cracker crumbs and sherry to the marshmallows. Keep stirring to combine.
3. Spread ¼ cup graham cracker crumbs in the bottom of a buttered loaf pan. Pour the marshmallow mixture over the crumbs. Chill in the refrigerator.
4. Serve with whipped cream.

Holy Cannoli Refrigerator Cake

Ingredients

- 1 package cream cheese (8 ounce)
- 1 container ricotta cheese (15 ounce)
- 1/2 cup sugar
- 1 tablespoon vanilla
- 2 semi-sweet chocolate baking squares , coarsely chopped
- 1 container COOL WHIP (8 ounce)
- 120 vanilla wafers
- 1 jar caramel topping (8 ounce)

Directions

1. Use an electric mixer to beat the cream cheese, ricotta cheese, sugar and vanilla in large bowl until well blended.
2. Stir in the chopped chocolate and mix well.
3. Stir in 2 cups of the COOL WHIP whipped topping.
4. Spread 2 cups of the mixture on the bottom of a 9" x 13" pan.
5. Place 30 wafers on the bottom of the pan. Drizzle caramel topping over the wafers. Add another layer of the whipped topping mixture.
6. Repeat with layers of wafers, caramel, and mixture until the wafers have all been used
7. Top with any remaining whipped topping.
8. Refrigerate for at least 4 hours before serving

Ice Box Fruit Cake

Ingredients

- 13 ounce jar marshmallow crème
- 1 box graham crackers
- 1 lb. candied cherries
- 1 lb. candied pineapple
- 14 ounce bag coconut
- 4 cup chopped pecans
- 1 cup white raisins
- 1/2 stick butter
- 1 can condensed milk

Directions

1. Melt the butter in a large saucepan using low heat.
2. Pour in condensed milk and marshmallow creme. Mix well and remove from heat.
3. Add the box of graham crackers, crushed.
4. Quarter the pineapple and cherries and add to the marshmallow mixture; mix well.
5. Mix in pecans, coconut and raisins. Mix all thoroughly.
6. Line 2 regular size loaf pans with saran wrap
7. Pack the cake mixture in the pan tightly.
8. Refrigerate until well chilled. Keep in refrigerator.

Lemon–Lime Refrigerator Poke Cake

Ingredients

- 3 ounces lime JELL-O gelatin
- 1 box instant lemon pudding mix (3 ounce)
- 1 envelope DREAM WHIP topping mix (1 1/3 ounce)
- 1 1/2 cups cold milk
- 1 teaspoon vanilla
- 1 box lemon cake mix (18 ounce)
- Eggs   (Use the amount specified in the cake mix directions)
- Oil   (Use the amount specified in the cake mix directions)
- Water (Use the amount specified in the cake mix directions)

Directions

1. Bake the lemon cake according to the directions on the box. Use a 9" x 13" cake pan.
2. While the cake is still warm poke holes into the top with the end of a wooden spoon or meat fork.
3. Mix the lime JELL-O with 3/4 cup hot water and stir. Then add 1/2 cup cold water.
4. Put the JELL-O mixture in the refrigerator until it gets slightly thick like syrup.
5. Pour the JELL-O into the holes in the cake and then all over the top. Make sure you get as much of the JELL-O mixture into the holes as you can.
6. Topping: Combine the dream whip, pudding mix, vanilla and milk together in a medium-sized bowl. Whip these ingredients for 5 minutes or until thick.
7. Spread the topping all over cake and refrigerate. Keep the cake chilled until you serve.

Lemon Pineapple Ice-Box Cake

Ingredients

- 14 graham crackers, crushed
- 1/2 cup white sugar
- 1/2 cup melted butter
- 1 can evaporated milk, chilled (12 fluid ounce)
- 1 cup white sugar
- 2 lemons, juiced
- 1 package lemon flavored gelatin (3 ounce)
- 1 cup crushed pineapple, drained
- 1/2 cup graham cracker crumbs
- 1/4 cup maraschino cherries, drained and chopped

Directions

Crust

1. Mix graham crackers, 1/2 cup sugar and melted butter and press into 9 x 13 inch pan.

Filling

1. Mix lemon gelatin with 1 cup boiling water and let cool.
2. Whip the chilled evaporated milk
3. Add the 1 cup sugar and lemon juice to the whipped evaporated milk. Whip until the sugar is dissolved.
4. Whip the cooled lemon gelatin into the milk mixture
5. Stir the pineapple into the milk mixture.
6. Pour the milk mixture over crust in pan.
7. Sprinkle with 1/2 cup crushed graham crackers and chopped maraschino cherries if desired.
8. Chill several hours or overnight in the refrigerator.

Lemon Snap Refrigerator Cake

Ingredients

- 30 round gingersnaps
- 1 cup low-fat milk
- 1 package lemon pudding mix (25 ounce)
- 1 ½ cups COOL WHIP

Directions

1. Combine the pudding mix and milk in a large bowl. Mix until smooth.
2. Fold the COOL WHIP into the pudding mixture and stir well. .
3. Scoop a generous teaspoon of the cream mixture and sandwich it between two gingersnaps.
4. Place the gingersnaps standing on edge at one end of a medium sized platter.
5. Create another gingersnap and cream "sandwich" as in step 3. This time also put some cream mixture on the top of the top cookie. Press this into the gingersnaps on your platter so it creates a small "log."
6. Repeat step 5 until you have a nice-sized gingersnap log. Make sure you reserve some of the cream mixture.
7. Use the remaining cream mixture to cover the entire log.
8. Refrigerate for a minimum of 8 hours.

Lime Refrigerator Cake

Ingredients

- 50 vanilla wafers
- 1 cup fresh lime juice
- 1 can sweetened condensed milk (14 ounce)
- 1 can evaporated milk (12 ounce)

Directions

1. Combine the condensed milk, evaporated milk and lime juice in a mixing bowl. Blend until well-mixed.
2. Place a layer of cookies in the bottom of a round 9" baking dish. Make sure the bottom is covered. Break up some cookies to fill in any gaps.
3. Spread about 1/5 of the milk and juice mixture over the cookies
4. Repeat the process of placing layers of cookies and the milk mixture until the ingredients run out. It's best if the top layer is the milk mixture.
5. Cover and refrigerate several hours or overnight.
6. When ready to serve cut into squares.

Variation

This cake is great when topped with fresh fruit.

Neapolitan Refrigerator Poke Cake

Ingredients

- 1 package fudge marble cake mix (18 ounce)
- 1 package strawberry JELL-O gelatin dessert (3 ounce)
- Eggs (Use the amount specified in the cake mix directions)
- Oil (Use the amount specified in the cake mix directions)
- 1 ½ cups milk
- 1 teaspoon vanilla
- 2 ½ cups frozen whipped topping , thawed
- 1 package instant vanilla pudding (3 ounce)

Directions

1. Mix the JELL-O by stirring it into 3/4 cup boiling water. Then add 1/2 cup cold water and stir.   Set the JELL-O mix aside and leave it at room temperature.
2. Mix the cake according to the directions on the package and bake in a 9"x13" pan.
3. When the cake is done remove it from the oven and cool for 30 minutes.
4. Poke deep holes about 1" apart into the top of the cake with a meat fork or a chopstick
5. Slowly pour all the JELL-O into the holes.
6. Refrigerate the cake
7. Topping: Combine the instant pudding, COOL WHIP, milk and vanilla. Blend until stiff and thick.
8. Frost the cake and refrigerate.
9. Serve chilled.

Orange Refrigerator Cake 1

Ingredients

- 4 cups fresh orange juice
- 1/3 cup lemon juice
- 2 (12 ounce) packages ladyfingers
- 1 cup heavy whipping cream
- 1 ½ cups white sugar
- 3 (.25 ounce) packages unflavored gelatin
- 1/8 teaspoon salt
- 1 cup diced orange segments
- 1 pint fresh strawberries

Directions

1. Line the bottom and sides of an 8 inch spring form pan with ladyfingers.
2. Mix 1 cup orange juice and the sugar in a saucepan. Heat and stir until the sugar is dissolved. Remove from heat.
3. Mix the gelatin in 1 cup of orange juice and then stir into the hot juice. Add the remaining 2 cups of orange juice, 1/3 cup lemon juice and the salt into the hot juice mixture. Chill until slightly thickened.
4. Whip the cream until stiff and then fold it into the orange juice and gelatin mixture. Gently mix in the orange sections.
5. Pour the mixture into the prepared pan. Chill for at least 4 hours. Remove sides of pan and place on a serving plate. Garnish the top with fresh strawberries.

Orange Refrigerator Cake 2

Ingredients

- 2 loaves angel food cake
- 1 package vanilla pudding mix (4 5/8 ounce)
- 1 envelope unflavored gelatin (1/4 ounce)
- 1 cup orange juice
- 1 tablespoon orange zest
- 2 cups heavy whipping cream , whipped

Directions

1. Mix the pudding using the directions on the package. Set aside.
2. Pour the orange juice into a small sauce pan. Sprinkle the gelatin over orange juice. Let it stand for 2 minutes.
3. Cook and stir over low heat until gelatin is dissolved.
4. Stir the orange juice–gelatin mixture into the pudding.
5. Add the orange zest.
6. Transfer to a large bowl. Cover and refrigerate for 2 hours or until cooled.
7. Slice one angel food cake in half width-wise.
8. Save one half for another use.
9. Cut remaining half into eight slices.
10. Cut second loaf into 16 slices.
11. Arrange half of the cake slices in an ungreased 13" x 9" x 2" dish.
12. Fold the whipped cream into the pudding. Spread half of the whipped cream mixture over the cake slices.
13. Repeat layers.
14. Cover and refrigerate overnight or until set.

Oreo Refrigerator Cake

Ingredients

- 1 bag OREO cookies , crushed, divided (15 ounce)
- 1 package cream cheese , softened (8 ounce)
- 1 package chocolate fudge instant pudding mix (6 ounce)
- 2 1/4 cups half-and-half cream (or use whole milk)
- 1/2 cup butter , melted
- 1 cup confectioners' sugar
- 1 container COOL WHIP , thawed (12 ounce)

Directions

1. Crush the OREO cookies.   Reserve 1/4 cup for topping.
2. Mix the remaining crushed cookies with the melted butter.
3. Press the cookie crumb mixture into the bottom of a greased 13" x 9" baking pan.
4. Combine the cream cheese with the confectioners' sugar in a bowl and mix on medium speed.
5. Fold in half of the COOL WHIP topping.
6. Spread the cream cheese-COOL WHIP mixture over cookie crumb layer.
7. Refrigerate 1/2 hour.
8. Put the milk and instant pudding mix in a bowl. Beat well until smooth.
9. Pour the pudding mixture over the chilled mixture in the pan.
10. Refrigerate for 1 hour.
11. Spread the rest of the COOL WHIP topping on top of pudding layer.
12. Sprinkle with remaining reserved cookie crumbs.
13. Put cake in the refrigerator, covered tightly.

Variations

- To reduce calories you can use low-fat cream cheese, low-fat COOL WHIP and skim milk
- For a different taste use French Vanilla or lemon pudding
- Another option is using a mixture of chocolate fudge pudding and vanilla pudding

Peppermint Refrigerator Cake

Ingredients

- 1/4 lb. peppermint stick candy
- 1 cup milk
- 2 teaspoons plain gelatin , soaked in 2 tablespoons water
- 1 cup whipping cream , whipped
- 12 ladyfingers or 12 slices sponge cakes

Directions

1. Crush the peppermint candy. Put the milk and crushed candy in a double boiler with the milk.
2. Heat to dissolve the candy.
3. Add the soaked gelatine and stir until dissolved.
4. Cool the mixture until it just begins to thicken.
5. Fold in the whipped cream.
6. Use waxed paper to line 2 sides and the bottom of a loaf pan. Let the waxed paper hang over the ends of the pan.
7. Arrange 4 lady fingers or sponge cake in the bottom of the pan.
8. Top with the peppermint cream mixture.
9. Repeat the layers topping it with lady fingers or sponge cake.
10. Chill until firm.
11. When you're ready to serve the cake use a spatula to loosen the ends. Use the edges of the paper to lift the cake and transfer it from the pan to a serving dish.

Pineapple Icebox Dessert

Ingredients

- 2 cups cold fat free milk
- 1 package sugar-free instant vanilla pudding mix (1 ounce)
- 1 cup reduced-fat whipped topping
- 1 can pineapple tidbits (20 ounce)
- 2 (3 ounce) packages ladyfingers

Directions

1. Combine the milk and pudding mix in a bowl and stir for 2 minutes.
2. Fold in the whipped topping and set it aside.
3. Drain the pineapple and reserve 1/4 cup juice.
4. Spread half of the ladyfingers in the bottom of an ungreased 11" x 7" x 2" dish.
5. Brush the ladyfingers with 2 tablespoons reserved pineapple juice.
6. Top the ladyfingers with half of the pudding mixture and half of the pineapple.
7. Repeat the layers of ladyfingers, pudding and pineapple.
8. Cover and refrigerate overnight.
9. Cut into squares.

Raspberry Icebox Cake

Ingredients

- 24 graham crackers, crushed
- 1/3 cup butter
- 1/4 cup packed brown sugar
- 1 package raspberry flavored gelatin mix (6 ounce)
- 1 cup boiling water
- 15 ounces frozen raspberries
- 20 large marshmallows
- 1/3 cup milk
- 1 cup heavy whipping cream, whipped

Directions

1. Preheat oven to 350 degrees.
2. Mix the butter, brown sugar and graham cracker crumbs until well mixed. Reserve 1/4 cup of this mixture for the topping. Use the remainder to create a crust by pressing it into the bottom of one 9" x 13" pan.
3. Bake at 350 degrees for 10 minutes. Then set aside to cool.
4. Dissolve raspberry gelatin in the boiling water. Add the frozen raspberries and stir until melted. Chill until partially set. Then spread the mixture over the crust.
5. Place the milk and marshmallows into a pan. Slowly heat until the marshmallows melt. Remove from heat and set aside to cool.
6. When cool fold in the whipped cream and spread on top of raspberry mixture. Sprinkle with remaining crumbs.
7. Chill for 3-4 hours before serving.

Strawberry Icebox Cake

Ingredients

- 2 cups pureed strawberries
- 6 cups of COOL WHIP (16oz. container)
- 12 graham crackers

Directions

1. Put 4 cups of COOL WHIP in a bowl and slowly fold in the pureed strawberries so that the mixture is blended well.
2. Line an 8"x8" pan with plastic wrap so that there are 2 inches outside the pan on all sides.
3. Put a layer of graham crackers in the bottom of the cake pan.
4. Spoon 1 ½ cups of the strawberry-COOL WHIP mixture on top of the graham crackers. Use the back of the spoon to smooth out the strawberry mixture.
5. Keep layering graham crackers and the strawberry-COOL WHIP mixture until you have used all 12 graham crackers.
6. Cover the cake and place it in the freezer and chill for 1 hour.
7. Remove the cake from freezer. Frost the cake with the remaining two cups of COOL WHIP.

Strawberry Refrigerator Poke Cake

Ingredients

- 1 package white or yellow cake mix (18 1/4 ounce)
- Eggs (Use the amount specified in the cake mix directions)
- Oil (Use the amount specified in the cake mix directions)
- Water (Use the amount specified in the cake mix directions)
- 2 (10 ounce) packages frozen strawberries, completely thawed and with the juice.
- 1 package vanilla pudding mix (3 1/2 ounce)
- 1 cup half-and-half cream
- 1/2 tablespoon cornstarch
- 1 container COOL WHIP frozen whipped topping , thawed (8 ounce)
- fresh sliced strawberries

Directions

1. Bake the cake according to package directions and bake in a 13" x 9" baking pan;   Set aside to cool to room temperature.
2. Using the handle of a wooden spoon poke holes in the top of the cake almost to the bottom. The holes should be about 1-inch apart. The more holes the better. Holes should be ¾" around.
3. Puree the thawed strawberries in a blender until smooth. Slowly drizzle the puree over the top of the cake concentrating on the holes.
4. Refrigerate for 2 hours.
5. Topping: Mix the pudding mix with 1 cup of half and half cream. Add in the 1/2 tablespoon cornstarch to the pudding mixture while mixing; Beat until smooth and thick.
6. Fold in the thawed COOL WHIP until combined.
7. Spread over the top of the cold cake
8. Arrange the fresh sliced strawberries on the top.
9. Refrigerate for 2 or more hours before serving.

Strawberry Refrigerator Cake

Ingredients

- 11 ounces crushed vanilla wafers
- 2 cups frozen strawberries (thawed)
- 1 box strawberry JELL-O (3 ounces)
- 1 cup chopped nuts
- 12 cups sugar
- 2 cups marshmallows
- 1 pint COOL WHIP
- 1 cup boiling water

Directions

1. Dissolve the JELL-O in boiling water.
2. Add sugar and marshmallows to the boiling water stirring until the marshmallows dissolve
3. Set aside until thickened.
4. Beat the marshmallow mixture with a mixer
5. Add the COOL WHIP and thawed strawberries.
6. Line the bottom of a 12" x 9" pan with crushed wafers.
7. Spread half of the strawberry mixture on top
8. Add another layer of wafers and another of the strawberry mixture
9. Top with a layer of crushed vanilla wafers
10. Sprinkle the chopped nuts on top
11. Chill in the refrigerator
12. Serve when well chilled.

Sweet Chocolate Refrigerator Cake

Ingredients

20 lady fingers

1/2 lb. sweet cooking chocolate

3 eggs, separated

1 teaspoon vanilla

1 cup whipping cream, divided

Directions

1. Line a straight sided loaf pan, 11" x 4" x 2 1/2" with wax paper.
2. Line the bottom of the pan with a row of 8 lady finger halves
3. Melt chocolate in a double boiler. Remove from heat.
4. Beat the egg whites until they form soft peaks and fold into the chocolate mixture
5. Whip 1/2 cup cream and fold into the chocolate mixture.
6. Spread 1/4 of the chocolate mixture on the ladyfingers in pan.
7. Add another row of lady fingers;
8. Repeat process until there are 4 layers of ladyfingers and chocolate mousse.
9. Top with a final row of ladyfingers.
10. Cover the cake with Saran Wrap.
11. Chill the cake for several hours or overnight.
12. Transfer to a cake dish and remove the Saran Wrap.
13. Whip remaining whip cream and use to frost sides of the cake.
14. Slice to serve.
15. Can be decorated with chocolate shavings.

Vanilla Refrigerator Cake

Ingredients

- 1 box vanilla wafers
- 2 containers COOL WHIP , thawed (8 ounce)
- 2 packages vanilla pudding , prepared to directions (6 ounce)

Directions

1. Line a Deep 13" x 9" pan with vanilla wafers.
2. Spread 1/3 of the pudding over the vanilla wafers.
3. Top with 1/3 of the COOL WHIP.
4. Repeat 2 more times. Top with COOL WHIP.
5. Cover and refrigerate overnight.

Variation

- You can use chocolate wafers and chocolate pudding

Other Books by Lori Burke

If you enjoyed this book you might also like Lori's latest book:

30 Delicious Icebox Cookie Recipes

23021496R00027

Made in the USA
San Bernardino, CA
31 July 2015